EDVARD GRIEG

Complete Lyric Pieces

for Piano

DOVER PUBLICATIONS, INC., NEW YORK

Published in Canada by General Publishing Company, Ltd., 30 Lesmill Road, Don Mills, Toronto, Ontario.

Published in the United Kingdom by Constable and Company, Ltd.

This Dover edition, first published in 1989, is a republication of ten works originally published separately by C. F. Peters, Leipzig, n.d., all with the title *Lyrische Stücke für Pianoforte*. The fingerings were provided by Adolf Ruthardt.

We are grateful to the Music Library of Wellesley College for the loan of the score.

Manufactured in the United States of America
Dover Publications, Inc., 31 East 2nd Street, Mineola, N.Y. 11501

Library of Congress Cataloging-in-Publication Data

Grieg, Edvard, 1843–1907.
[Piano music. Selections]
Complete lyric pieces : for piano / Edvard Grieg.
p. of music.
Reprint. Originally published: Leipzig : C.F. Peters (pl. no.: 8460, 6729, 6954, 7206, 7637, 7840–7841, 8184–8185, 8355–8356, 8567, 8773).
Contents: Op. 12 (1867)—Op. 38 (1884)—Op. 43 (1886)—Op. 47 (1888)—Op. 54 (1891)—Op. 57 (1893)—Op. 62 (1895)—Op. 65 (1897)—Op. 68 (1899)—Op. 71 (1901).
ISBN 0-486-26176-X
1. Piano music. I. Title. II. Title: Lyric pieces.
M22.G84D7 1989 89-35305
CIP
M

Contents

Complete Lyric Pieces

8 LYRIC PIECES, OP. 12

1. Arietta

Poco Andante e sostenuto.

2. Waltz
Vals — Walzer

p
ritard.
a tempo
ritard.
f
pp
f ritard.
p
Coda.
p dolce
pp
Ped.

3. Watchman's Song

Vaegtersang — Wächterlied

(composed after a performance of Shakespeare's *Macbeth*)

pp
Ped.
pp
Ped.
f
pp
Ped.
p
ritard.

4. Elves' Dance

Elverdans (Alfedans) — Elfentanz

pp
f
cresc.
fz
ppp

5. Folk Melody

Folkevise — Volksweise

morendo
mf
morendo

6. Norwegian Melody

Norsk — Norwegisch

fz
pp
fz
fz
fz
fz
fz
fz
fz
fz
fz
fz
fz
fz
ff
fz
sempre ritard.
fz
fz

7. Album Leaf

Stambogsblad (Albumblad) — Albumblatt

sosten.
fz
Ped.

8. National Song

Faedrelandssang — Vaterländisches Lied

Maestoso.

8 LYRIC PIECES, OP. 38

1. Berceuse

Vuggevise

Allegretto tranquillo. ♩= 92.

Con moto.
p tre corde
rit.
a tempo
p
Ped.
ritard.
Ped.
più p
una corda
Ped.
a tempo
pp
tre corde
Ped.
cresc. e stretto
Ped.

f
dim. e ritard. molto
a tempo
p
pp
morendo
ppp

2. Folk Melody

Folkevise — Volksweise

Allegro con moto. ♩= 144.

sempre cresc.
f
dim.
poco
a
poco
rit.
p a tempo
cresc.
f
p
dimin.
e
rit.
pp

3. Melody
Melodie

a tempo
p
Ped.
cresc. poco e stretto
rit.
a tempo
pp

4. Halling
(Norwegian Dance)

a tempo
f
p
pp
Ped.
*
pp
rit.
Ped.
*
a tempo
fp
poco rit. pp

5. Leaping Dance

Springdans — Springtanz

ff
p
dim.
poco
a
poco
pp

6. Elegy
Elegie

Allegretto semplice. ♩= 80.

fp
cantabile
cresc.
pp
fp
mf
p

7. Waltz

Vals — Walzer

Tempo I.
p
ritard.
p a tempo
cresc.
f
p
ri - tar - dan - do
Lento.

8. Canon

Kanon

Piu mosso, ma tranquillo. ♩ = 126.
p
Ped.
pp
cresc.
mf
cresc.
f
p
dim.
Minore Da Capo al Fine.

6 LYRIC PIECES, OP. 43

1. Butterfly

Sommerfugl — Schmetterling

una corda
pp
ritard.
a tempo
dolce
cresc. poco a poco
con moto e poco stretto
tre corde
f
dim.
p

ritard.
pp una corda
a tempo
dolce
cresc. poco a poco
poco stretto
tre corde
f
ffz
dim. e rit.
p
pp

2. Lonely Wanderer

Ensom Vandrer — Einsamer Wanderer

poco ritard.
a tempo
poco rit.
a tempo
poco ritard.
a tempo
rit.

3. In My Homeland

I Hjemmet — In der Heimath

poco più mosso
cresc.
f ritard.
Tempo I.
pp
p
ppp
Ped.

4. Little Bird

Liden Fugl — Vöglein

cresc.
f
p
pp
ppp
poco ritar - - dan - - - - do

5. Erotic Piece

Erotik

più mosso e sempre stretto
cresc.
più cresc.
Tempo I.
f ri - tar - dan - do mol - to
p
dolce
più p e tranquillo
ri - tar - dan - do
pp

6. To Spring

Til Foråret — An den Frühling

cresc.
m.d.
agitato.
m.d.
m.s.
più f
più f
ritard.
ff
Tempo I.
p e dolce
m.d.
p

animato
poco rit.
a tempo
cresc.
poco rit.
a tempo
dim.
cresc.
dim.

cresc. molto
f
sosten.
cresc. molto
f
sosten.
ritard.
ff
p a tempo
dim. e rit. poco a poco
ritard.
ff
p a tempo
una corda
dim. e rit. poco a poco
pp a tempo
pp a tempo
ritard.
8
m.d.
m.s.
Lento.
più rit.
ppp

7 LYRIC PIECES, OP. 47

1. Valse-Impromptu

m.s.
m.s.
Tempo I.
p
pp
f
sempre
f
pp
poco
tranquillo
ritard.
a tempo
p
rubato
cresc.
rubato

fz

pp

stretto molto e cresc.

f rit.

molto

molto più lento

cantabile

m. s.

p

pp

Ped.

Tempo I.

pp

f

sempre

f

pp

poco

tr
tranquillo
ritard.
a tempo
p
rubato
cresc.
rubato
fz
pp
stretto molto e cresc.
f
rit.
molto
molto più
cantabile
lento
m. s.
p
m. s.
pp
ppp
Ped.

2. Album Leaf

Albumblad — Albumblatt

Ped.
più cresc.
ten.
ff
dim.
molto
dolcissimo
pp una corda
m.d.
m.s.
tre corde
f
poco rit.
a tempo
p e dolce
cresc.

dim.
cantabile.
cresc.
più cresc.
ten.
dim.

molto
dolcissimo
pp una corda
m.s.
m.d.
tre corde
f m.s.
m.d.
poco rit.
a tempo
p e dolce
cresc.
f
f
dim.
p
pp

3. Melody
Melodie

ff
ffz dim. molto
e meno mosso poco a poco
Tempo I.
poco
rit.
p
f
dim.
più mosso
pp
stretto
f

più f
ff
ffz dim. molto e meno mosso
poco a poco
poco rit.
Tempo I.
p
f
dim.
dim.
sempre
ritard.
pp
morendo

4. Halling
(Norwegian Dance)

5. Melancholy

Melankoli — Melancholie

molto
ffz
a tempo
p
un poco più mosso
cresc.
f
p
cresc.
più cresc.
f
ritard.
molto
ffz
a tempo
p
dim.
pp

6. Leaping Dance
Springdans — Springtanz

Ped.
p
pp
cresc.
molto
ff
dim.
ppp

7. Elegy

Elegie

poco mosso.
espressivo
cresc. ed
agitato
Ped.
Ped.
Tempo I.
rit.
Ped.
p
morendo
pp
Ped.

6 LYRIC PIECES, OP. 54

1. Shepherd Boy

Gjaetergut — Hirtenknabe

ff
dim. e
rallent.
più dim. e ritard.
Ped.
Tempo I.
molto
ppp
p
molto tranquillo ed espressivo
pp
agitato
molto
ff
dim.
e più tranquillo
p
dim.
pp
cantabile
p
pp

2. Peasants' March

Gangar — Norwegischer Bauernmarsch

sempre ppp
Ped. sempre
cresc.
molto
f
più f
ff
fff
dimin.

p tranquillo
f
p
ff
p
dimin.
sempre
ppp
Ped. sempre
sempre ppp

cresc.
molto
f
più f
ff
fff
dim.
p tranquillo
dim. e poco rit.
pp
Ped. al Fine

3. March of the Trolls

Troldtog — Zug der Zwerge

dim. poco a poco
p
dim.
una corda
pp

p cantabile
p
Ped.
Ped.
Ped.
Ped.
pp
Ped.

p
p
dim.
Ped.

pp
staccato
sempre pp
staccato
staccato
cresc. poco
una corda
tre corde
a poco
molto
ff

dim. poco a poco
p
dim.
una corda
pp
ff

4. Notturno

p a tempo
poco
p
poco
Più mosso.
pp
Ped. una corda
ppp
poco a poco
cresc.
molto
ff
Ped. tre corde
poco rit.

p
a tempo
cresc.
molto
f
ff
Ped.

dim. sempre
Ped.
poco rit.
a tempo
p
morendo
Adagio.
pp

5. Scherzo

Prestissimo leggiero.

più p
dim.
pp
morendo
poco
ppp
Più tranquillo.
p cantabile
cresc.
f

fp
fp
fp
fp
pp
una corda
tre corde
cresc.
f
Tempo I.
pp
una corda
sempre pp

feroce
f
Ped.
ff
Ped.
Ped.
p dolce
Ped.
dim.
Ped.
più p
dim.
pp
Ped.
Ped.
morendo
poco
Ped.
Ped.
ppp
Ped.

6. Bell-Ringing

Klokkeklang — Glockengeläute

sempre più cresc.
molto
fff
dim. molto e poco ritard.
Tempo I.
pp
dim.
pp
molto
ffz
p
pp
morendo

6 LYRIC PIECES, OP. 57

1. Vanished Days

Svundne Dage — Entschwundene Tage

Ped.
pp una corda
tre corde
cresc.
più cresc.
molto
f
ff
Adagio.
poco dim. e molto rit.
p
pp

Allegro vivace.
p dolce e leggiero
Ped.
p
Ped.
p
f
p
molto
cresc. e stretto
f
fz
Più lento.
pp
Ped.

Molto vivo.
(longa)
ff
p
f
p
f
p
molto cresc. e stretto
f
fz
Più lento.
pp
Molto vivo.
(longa)
ff
p

poco a poco cresc.

Ped.
pp una corda
tre corde
cresc.
più cresc.
molto
f
ff
poco dim. e molto rit.
Adagio.
p
pp

2. Gade

cresc.
più cresc.
dim. e
sempre poco più tranquillo
p dolce
dim.
ritard.

a tempo
p
mf
p
mf
p
cresc.
più cresc.
f
dim. e sempre poco più tranquillo

p
dolce
f
dim.
ritard.
a tempo
cresc.
ff
molto
fz
dim.
pp
m.d.
m.s.

3. Illusion

p
f
p
f
pp
p più tranquillo
sempre ritard.

a tempo
p
dim. e rit.
pp
p
f

p
f
pp
p più tranquillo
sempre ritard.
a tempo
p
dim. e rit.
pp

4. Secret

Hemmelighed — Geheimniss

Più mosso.
pp
pp stretto poco a poco
Ped.
ppp

Tempo I. ma recitando.
p
cresc.
più cresc.
f
rit.
poco a poco a tempo
pp
dolce
Ped.
f

Più mosso.
pp
pp stretto poco a poco
Ped.
ppp

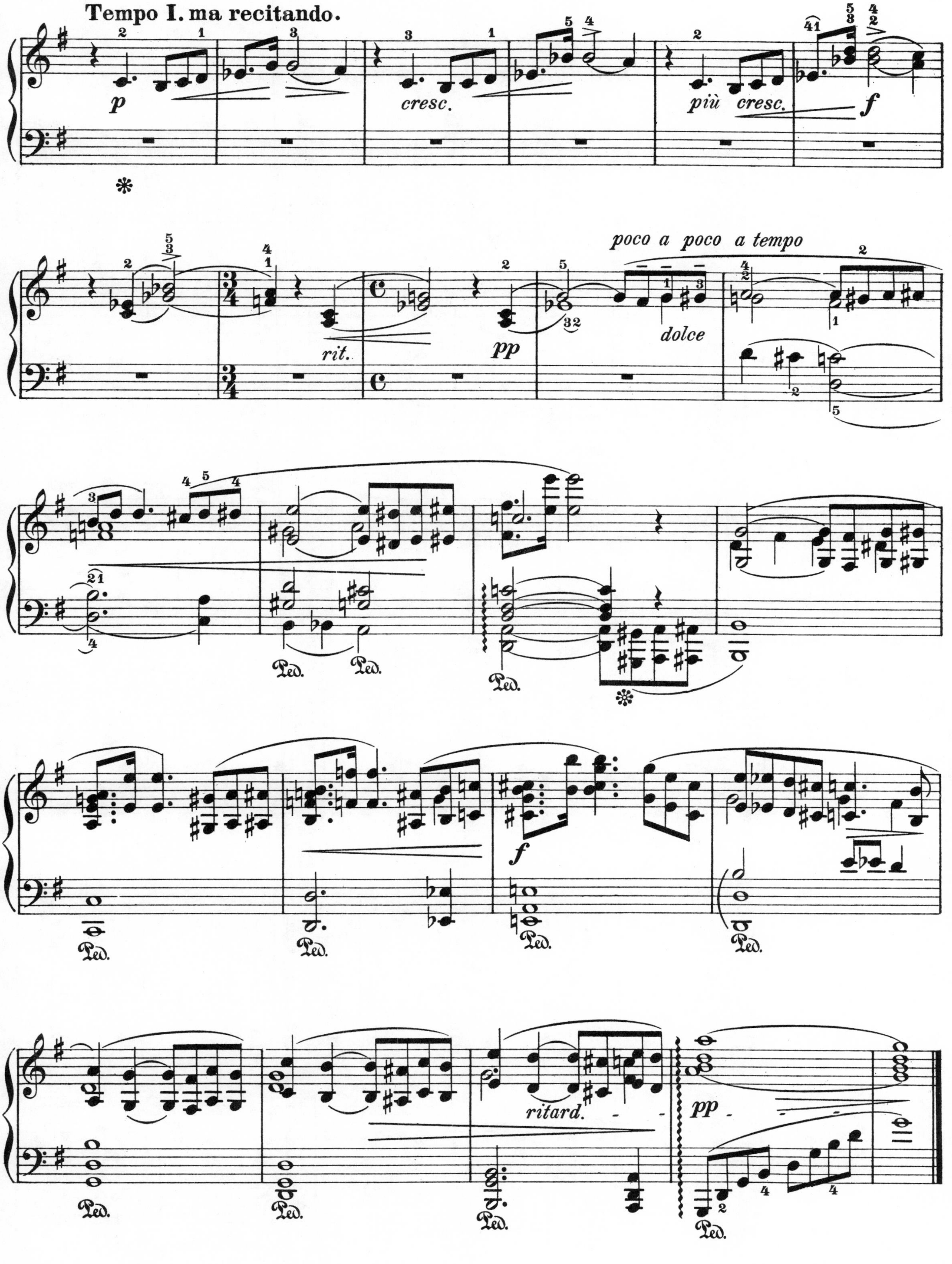

Tempo I. ma recitando.

p

cresc.

più cresc.

f

rit.

pp

poco a poco a tempo

dolce

f

ritard.

pp

5. She Dances

Hun danser — Sie tanzt

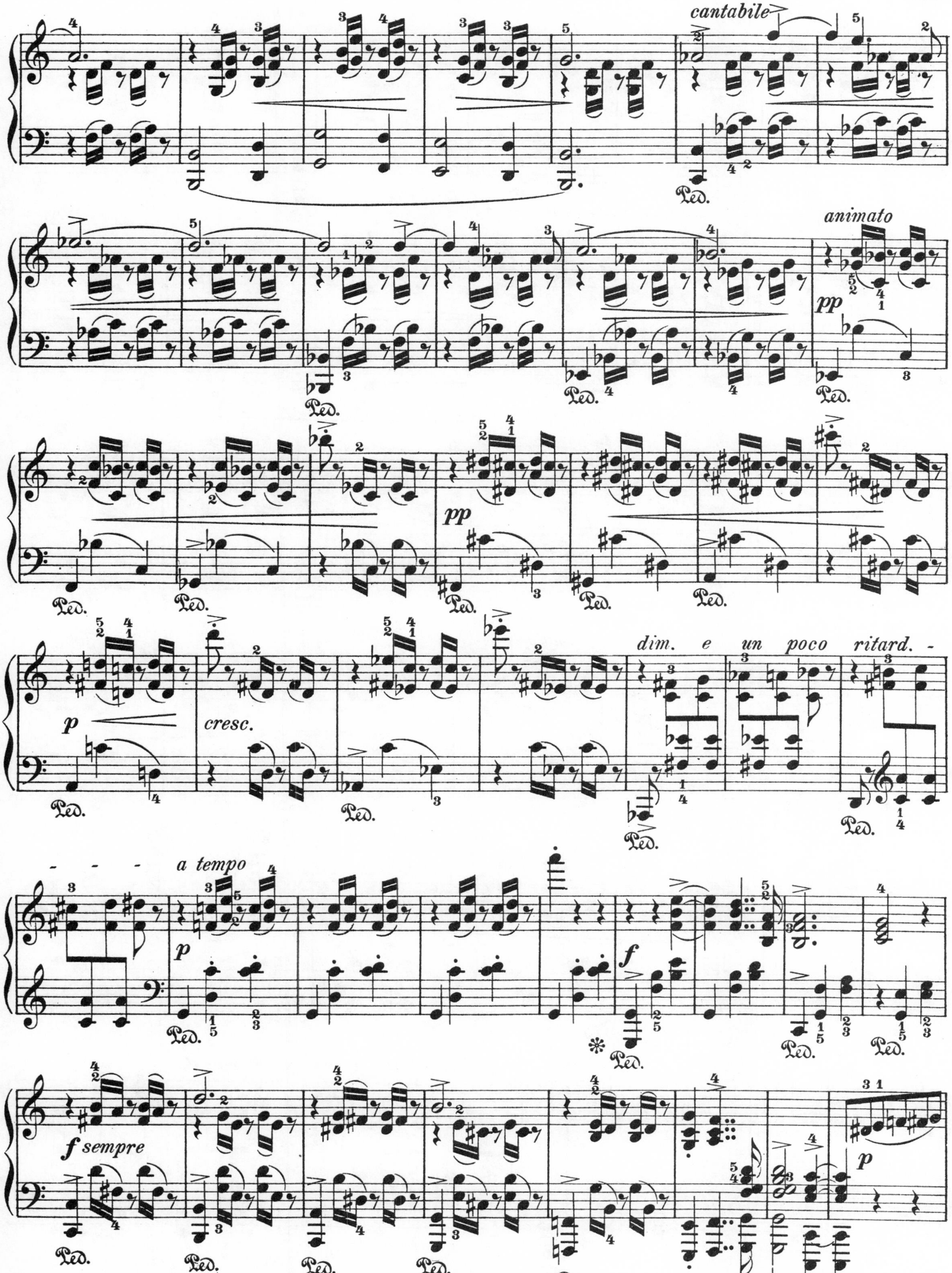

cantabile

animato

pp

pp

p

cresc.

dim. e un poco ritard. - - - - *a tempo*

p

f

f sempre

p

cantabile
p dolce
Ped.
Ped.
Ped.
cantabile
Ped.
Ped.
animato
pp
Ped.
Ped.
Ped.
Ped.
pp
Ped.
Ped.
Ped.
p
Ped.
cresc.
dim. e un poco ritard.
Ped.
Ped.
Ped.

a tempo
p
Ped.
f
f sempre
più vivo
dim.
pp
due Ped. al Fine.

6. Homesickness

Hjemve — Heimweh

Molto più vivo.
pp una corda
Ped.
fz
poco
fp
Ped.
fp

fp
fp
fz
poco
fp
Ped.
fp
fp
fp

Tempo I.
rit.
longa
p
pp
poco a poco più lento al Fine.
rit.

6 LYRIC PIECES, OP. 62

1. Sylph

Sylfide — Sylphe

pp
Ped.
string.
cresc.
f vivacissimo
Tempo I.
p
sempre
8

poco rit.
a tempo
poco rit.
a tempo
poco rit.
a tempo

pp
cresc.
più cresc.
f
ff
dim. poco
a poco
pp
ppp

2. Thanks
Tak — Dank

pp
Ped.
cresc. e stretto
più cresc.
f
rit.
fz
p
a
tempo

poco cresc.
pp
cresc. e stretto
più cresc.
f
rit.
fz
p
a

tempo
poco cresc.
Ped.
ri - tar - dan - do
ben ten.
m.g.
m.g.
m.g.
f
p

3. French Serenade

Fransk Serenade — Französische Serenade

cresc.
scherzando
pp
p
cresc.
p
cresc.

f
p
Ped.
cresc.
pp scherzando
cresc.
p

cresc.
f
p
pp scherzando
ppp

4. The Brook

Baekken — Bächlein

pp
cresc.
f
fz
dim.

pp
cresc.
f
pp
pp
cresc.

f
fz
dim.
pp
cresc.
f
pp

stretto
rfz
pp
Ped.
Ped.

5. Phantom

Drömmesyn — Traumgesicht

tr
Ped.
Ped.
Ped.
Ped.
dim.
pp
p
Ped.
Ped.
Ped.
pp
2 Ped.
Ped.
pp
2 Ped.

6. Homeward

Hjemad — Heimwärts

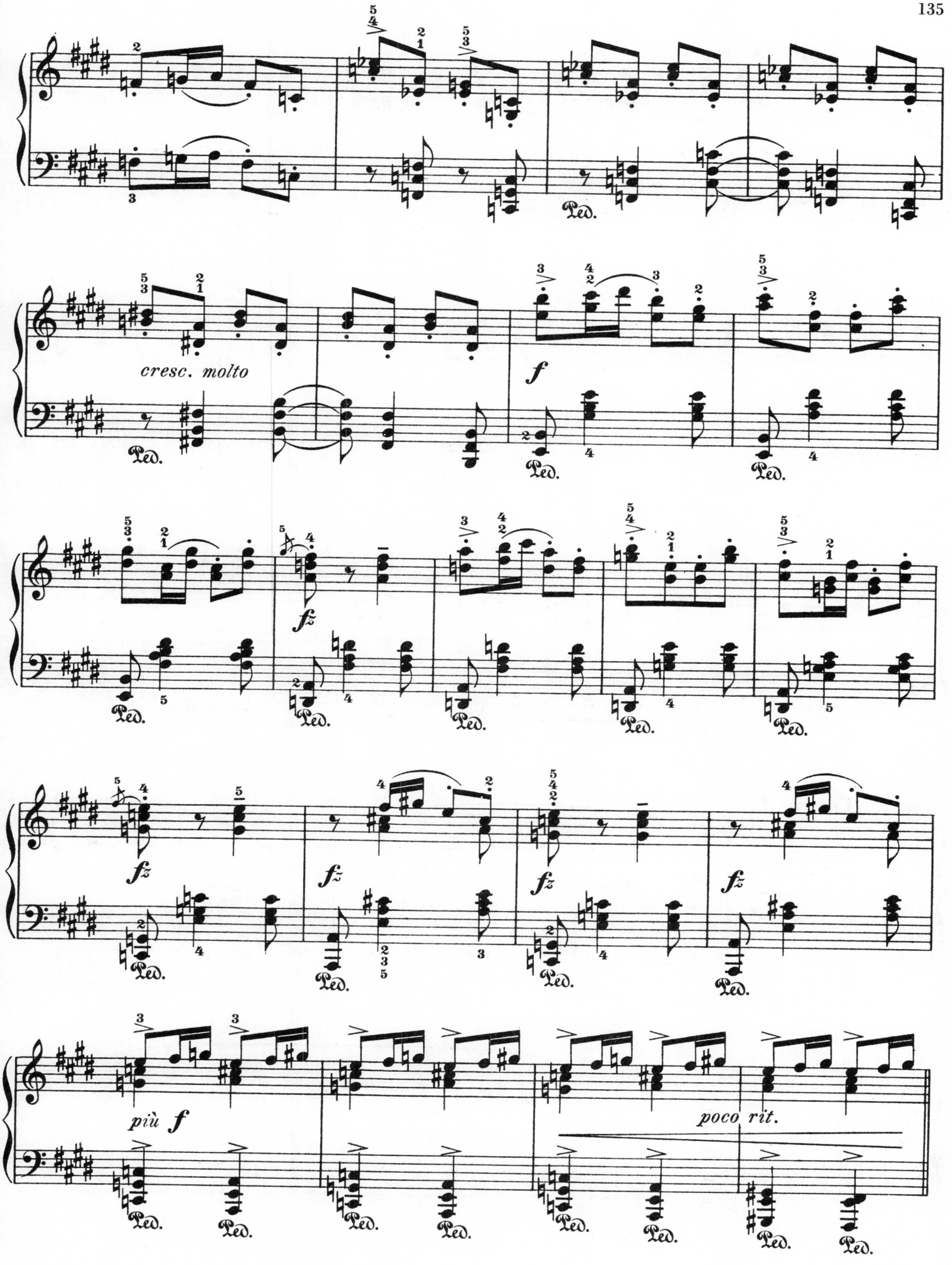

cresc. molto

f

fz

più f

poco rit.

Molto Allegro.
ff
Ped.
stretto
Tempo I.
p cantabile

poco rit.

a tempo
pp
Ped.
pp sempre
cresc. poco a poco
cresc. molto

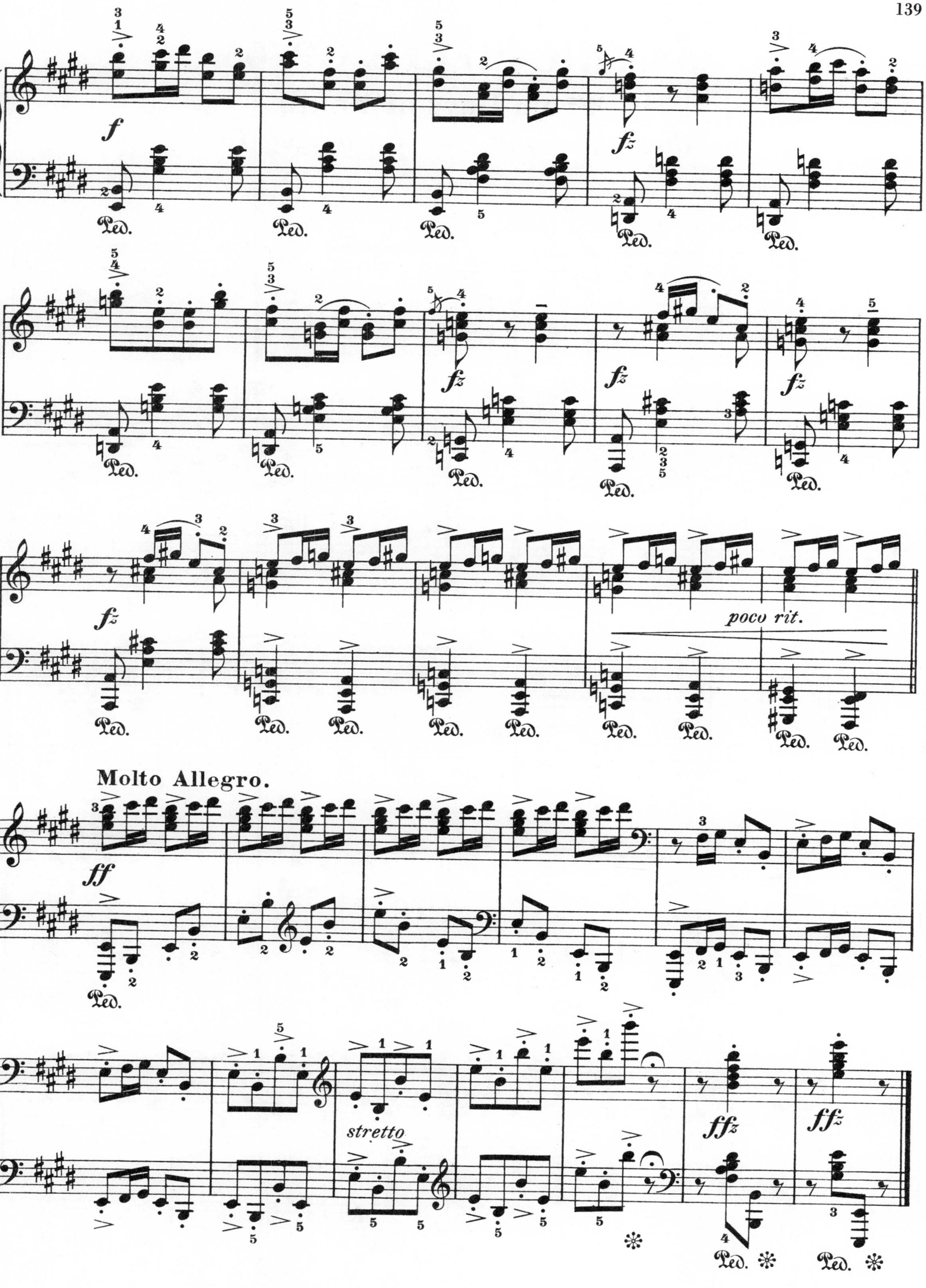
f
Ped.
fz
poco rit.
Molto Allegro.
ff
stretto
ffz

6 LYRIC PIECES, OP. 65

1. From Days of Youth

Fra Ungdomsdagene — Aus jungen Tagen

più cresc.
a tempo
m.d.
più f
dim.

dim.
pp
poco rit.
Molto più vivo.
pp
una corda
pp
senza Ped.
cresc.
tre corde
più cresc.
ff

ff
Ped.
p
dim.

pp
Ped.
1
Tempo I.
p cant.
p

cresc.
stretto
più cresc.
a tempo
f
m.d.
più f
ff

ffz
Ped.
Ped.
ffz
Ped.
Ped.
dim.
Ped.
p
Ped.

dim.
Ped.
Ped.

Ped.
Ped.
Ped.

pp
ppp
Ped.
Ped.

poco rit.
f
rit. p
Ped.
Ped.

2. Peasant's Song

Bondens Sang — Lied des Bauers

f
p
dim.
pp
meno p
cresc.
più cresc.
f
p
dim.
pp
dim.
ppp

3. Sadness
Tungsind — Schwermuth

dim. e rit.
a tempo
cresc.
string.
rall.
a tempo
cresc.
string.
più
Allegro agitato.

Meno Allegro.
dim.
e
rit.
Tempo I.
p
Ped.
cresc. e stretto
f
dim. molto e rit. pp
a tempo
p
cresc.
string.
f
rall.
a tempo
p

cresc.
string.
più f
ff
Allegro agitato.
Meno Allegro.
dim.
e
rit.
Tempo I.
p
Ped.
cresc. e stretto
f
dim. molto e rit. pp

4. Salon

tranquillo
p
con moto
p
pp
rit.
a tempo
p dolce
p

cresc.
e
string.
f
1
tranquillo
p
con moto
p
pp

rit.
p dolce
p
cresc.
string.
f
tranquillo
p

5. In Ballad Style

I Balladetone — Im Balladenton

un poco mosso
pp
cresc.
f
pp
cresc.
f
dim. e rit.
Tempo I.
pp
cresc. molto
ff
dim.
p
un poco mosso
pp

cresc.
f
pp
cresc.
poco rit.
Tempo I.
f
p
cresc. molto
ff
dim. e rit.
p
pp

6. Wedding Day at Troldhaugen*

Bryllupsdag på Troldhaugen — Hochzeitstag auf Troldhaugen

*Troldhaugen, site of the composer's country villa.

sempre pp
Ped.
f
Ped.
dim.
pp dolce
Ped.
una corda
Ped.
f
tre corde
Ped.
dim.
pp
una corda
Ped.
pp sempre
Ped. sempre

Ped.
cresc.
Ped.
tre corde
poco a poco
Ped.
più cresc.
Ped.
Ped.
f

marc.
più f
poco rit.
a tempo
fff
fz
Ped.

Poco tranquillo.
cantando
p
Ped.
cantando
f
dolce
pp
una corda
dolce
pp

p
Ped.
f
tre corde
Tempo I.

pp
una corda
sempre
pp
f
dim.
pp
dolce
una corda
f
tre corde

dim.
pp
dolce
una corda
pp sempre
sempre
cresc.
tre corde
più cresc.
f

Ped.
marc.
più f
poco rit.
a tempo fff
fff sempre

staccato sempre
p
dim.
sopra
pp
ppp
fffz
una corda
tre corde

6 LYRIC PIECES, OP. 68

1. Sailors' Song

Matrosernes Opsang — Matrosenlied

cresc.
poco ritard.
a tempo
ma ben ten.
ff
poco a poco ritard.
p
cresc.
poco ritard.
a tempo
ma ben ten.
ff
poco a poco ritard.

2. Grandmother's Minuet

Bedstemors Menuet — Grossmutters Menuett

con moto
pp
un poco stretto
fz
un poco rit.

Tempo I.
pp
pp al fine
ritard.
con moto
pp

un poco stretto
fz
un poco rit.
Tempo I.
pp
Ped.
pp al fine
ritard.

3. At Your Feet

For dine Fødder — Zu deinen Füssen

Più mosso.
p cantab.
stretto
cresc.
agitato
f
dim. e rall.
a tempo
p la melodia ben ten.
cresc. molto
f
dim. molto
poco rit.

a tempo, ma agitato
p
pp
cresc. e string.
più cresc. e molto appassionato
Pedal sempre
ff
poco rit.
Tempo I.
cantab. e ben ten.
pp

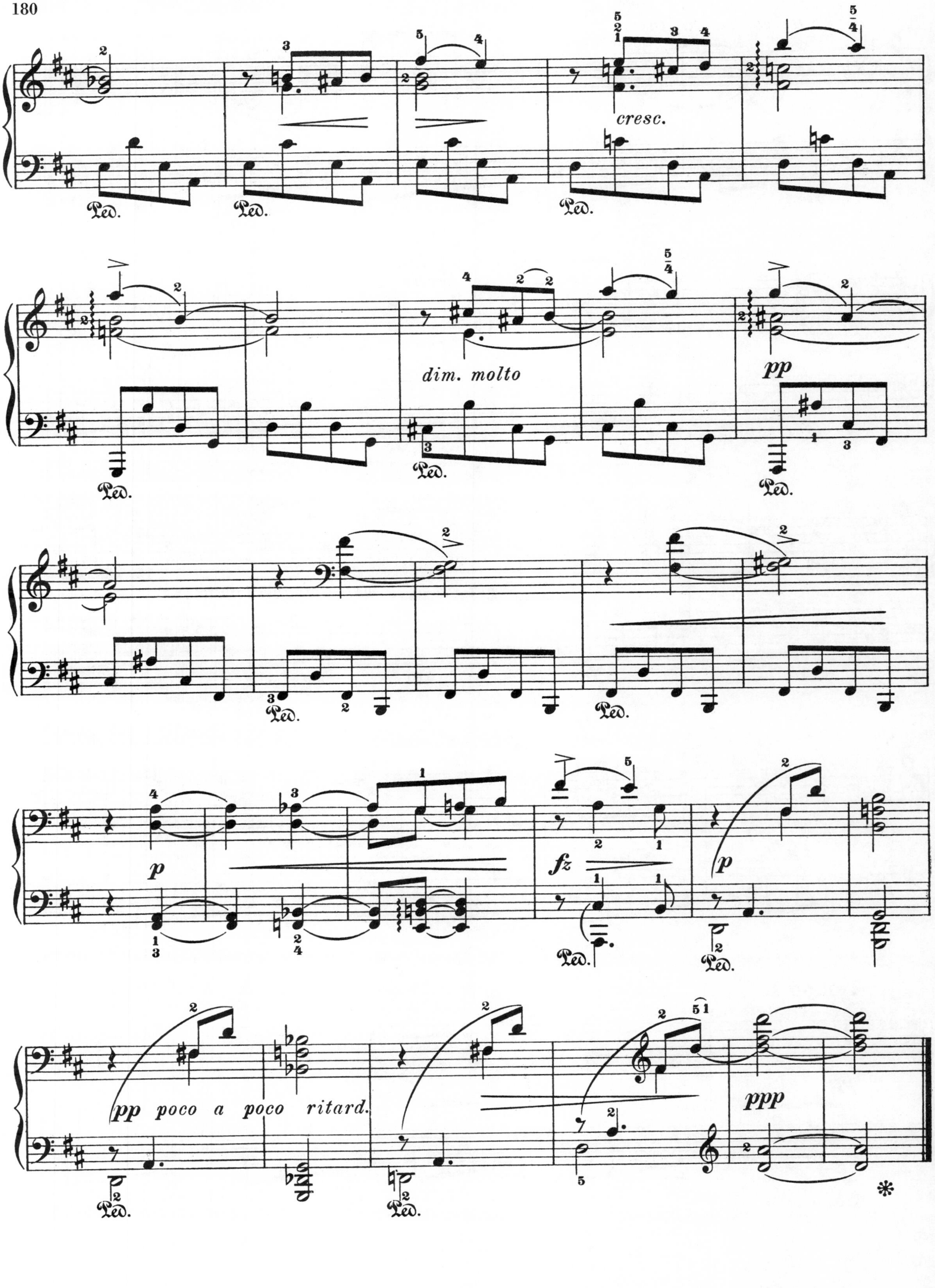

cresc.

dim. molto

pp

p

fz

p

pp poco a poco ritard.

ppp

4. Evening in the Mountains

Aften på Höjfeldet — Abend im Hochgebirge

Tempo I.
cresc.
f
più f e ten.
agitato
ff
dim.
molto e più
tranq.
p
ritard.
a tempo tranq.
p
poco rit.
a tempo
ff
m.s.
rit.
p
pp

5. Cradle Song

Bådnlåt — An der Wiege

cresc. molto
fz
Ped.
p
una corda
Ped.
ppp
poco rit.
a tempo
p
cresc.
molto
fz
poco rit.
molto
a tempo
p la melodia ben ten.
dim. e rit.
pp
ppp
Ped.
Ped. al Fine.

6. Valse mélancolique

a tempo
p
animato
pp
Ped.
cresc.
e stretto
poco a poco
più stretto
ffz
Ped. sempre

Tempo I.
tranq.
rit. molto
p
Ped.
cresc.
Ped.
f
dim. e rit.
p a tempo
poco rit.
pp
a tempo
cresc. e stretto
f
ff

a tempo
p
animato
pp
Ped.
cresc.
e stretto
poco a poco
Ped. sempre
più stretto
ffz

Tempo I.
tranq.
rit. molto
p
Ped.
cresc.
f
dim.e rit.
p a tempo
poco rit.
pp
a tempo

cresc.e stretto
f
ff
p
dim.
pp

7 LYRIC PIECES, OP. 71

1. Once upon a Time

Der var engang — Es war einmal

Allegro brioso. 𝅗𝅥. wie vorher 𝅘𝅥
(Im norwegischen Springtanzton)
pp
Ped.
p
pp
una corda
8
8
cresc.
tre corde

più cresc.
f
più f poco a poco
poco
ritard.
ff a tempo

1
p
dim.
1
pp
1
ppp
Andante.
(Wie zu Anfang.)
p
ani-
pp
f
mato
fz
dim. e rit. molto pp
a tempo
tranquillo
pp rit. e morendo al fine.
ppp

2. Summer Evening
Sommeraften — Sommerabend

Tempo I.
p dolce
più p
poco mosso
p
cresc. e stretto
Ped.
più cresc.
e stretto
Ped.
f
Tempo I.
p dolce
più p

3. Little Troll

Småtrold — Kobold

pp
cresc.
più cresc.
f
pp
dolce
cresc. molto
f
p

dim.
pp
pp sempre
ff
1
pp
ff
ffz
Ped.

4. Woodland Peace

Skovstilhed — Waldesstille

a tempo

p

p

p

dim.

pp

cresc. e stretto molto

f

Ped.

8

3

3

3

3

m.s.

Tempo I.
pp
Ped.
Ped.
p
poco rit.
a tempo
stretto
tranquillo
p
stretto
tranquillo
ten.
p

rall.
fz
a tempo
tranquillo
pp
una corda
molto cresc. e stretto
tre corde
f
ffz
p
slentando
tranquillo
molto tranquillo
ppp
una corda
pp
morendo
più lento
ppp

5. Halling

(Norwegian Dance)

f
pp
Ped.
f
pp
Ped.
cresc. poco a
poco
più cresc.
f
Ped.
Ped.

Ped.
più f
Ped.
glissando
ff
Ped.
Ped.
(segue)
p

pp
dim.
Wiederholung ad lib.
1.
2.
ppp
calando
Allegro molto.
(Doppio movimento)
p
cresc.
f
Tempo I.
8
fff marcatissimo
trem.
Ped.

6. Gone

Forbi — Vorüber

(In memoriam)

cresc.
più cresc.
f
rit.
a tempo
p
f
ben ten.
ritard.
molto
ffz
molto
p

7. Remembrances*

Efterklang — Nachklänge

*Compare "Arietta," Op. 12, No. 1.

pp
pp
cresc.
cresc. molto
f
poco rit.
(poco)
a tempo
p
cantabile
rit. al fine
ppp
Ped.

Dover Piano and Keyboard Editions

THE WELL-TEMPERED CLAVIER: Books I and II, Complete, Johann Sebastian Bach. All 48 preludes and fugues in all major and minor keys. Authoritative Bach-Gesellschaft edition. Explanation of ornaments in English, tempo indications, music corrections. 208pp. 9⅜ × 12¼. 24532-2 Pa. **$8.95**

KEYBOARD MUSIC, J. S. Bach. Bach-Gesellschaft edition. For harpsichord, piano, other keyboard instruments. English Suites, French Suites, Six Partitas, Goldberg Variations, Two-Part Inventions, Three-Part Sinfonias. 312pp. 8⅛ × 11. 22360-4 Pa. **$10.95**

ITALIAN CONCERTO, CHROMATIC FANTASIA AND FUGUE AND OTHER WORKS FOR KEYBOARD, Johann Sebastian Bach. Sixteen of Bach's best-known, most-performed and most-recorded works for the keyboard, reproduced from the authoritative Bach-Gesellschaft edition. 112pp. 9 × 12. 25387-2 Pa. **$7.95**

COMPLETE KEYBOARD TRANSCRIPTIONS OF CONCERTOS BY BAROQUE COMPOSERS, Johann Sebastian Bach. Sixteen concertos by Vivaldi, Telemann and others, transcribed for solo keyboard instruments. Bach-Gesellschaft edition. 128pp. 9⅜ × 12¼. 25529-8 Pa. **$7.95**

ORGAN MUSIC, J. S. Bach. Bach-Gesellschaft edition. 93 works. 6 Trio Sonatas, German Organ Mass, Orgelbüchlein, Six Schubler Chorales, 18 Choral Preludes. 357pp. 8⅛ × 11. 22359-0 Pa. **$12.95**

COMPLETE PRELUDES AND FUGUES FOR ORGAN, Johann Sebastian Bach. All 25 of Bach's complete sets of preludes and fugues (i.e. compositions written as pairs), from the authoritative Bach-Gesellschaft edition. 168pp. 8⅜ × 11. 24816-X Pa. **$9.95**

TOCCATAS, FANTASIAS, PASSACAGLIA AND OTHER WORKS FOR ORGAN, J. S. Bach. Over 20 best-loved works including Toccata and Fugue in D minor, BWV 565; Passacaglia and Fugue in C minor, BWV 582, many more. Bach-Gesellschaft edition. 176pp. 9 × 12. 25403-8 Pa. **$9.95**

TWO- AND THREE-PART INVENTIONS, J. S. Bach. Reproduction of original autograph ms. Edited by Eric Simon. 62pp. 8⅛ × 11. 21982-8 Pa. **$7.95**

THE 36 FANTASIAS FOR KEYBOARD, Georg Philipp Telemann. Graceful compositions by 18th-century master. 1923 Breslauer edition. 80pp. 8⅛ × 11. 25365-1 Pa. **$4.95**

GREAT KEYBOARD SONATAS, Carl Philipp Emanuel Bach. Comprehensive two-volume edition contains 51 sonatas by second, most important son of Johann Sebastian Bach. Originality, rich harmony, delicate workmanship. Authoritative French edition. Total of 384pp. 8⅜ × 11¼.
Series I 24853-4 Pa. **$8.95**
Series II 24854-2 Pa. **$8.95**

KEYBOARD WORKS/Series One: Ordres I–XIII; Series Two: Ordres XIV–XXVII and Miscellaneous Pieces, François Couperin. Over 200 pieces. Reproduced directly from edition prepared by Johannes Brahms and Friedrich Chrysander. Total of 496pp. 8⅛ × 11.
Series I 25795-9 Pa. **$9.95**
Series II 25796-7 Pa. **$9.95**

KEYBOARD WORKS FOR SOLO INSTRUMENTS, G. F. Handel. 35 neglected works from Handel's vast oeuvre, originally jotted down as improvisations. Includes Eight Great Suites, others. New sequence. 174pp. 9⅜ × 12¼. 24338-9 Pa. **$8.95**

WORKS FOR ORGAN AND KEYBOARD, Jan Pieterszoon Sweelinck. Nearly all of early Dutch composer's difficult-to-find keyboard works. Chorale variations; toccatas, fantasias; variations on secular, dance tunes. Also, incomplete and/or modified works, plus fantasia by John Bull. 272pp. 9 × 12. 24935-2 Pa. **$11.95**

ORGAN WORKS, Dietrich Buxtehude. Complete organ works of extremely influential pre-Bach composer. Toccatas, preludes, chorales, more. Definitive Breitkopf & Härtel edition. 320pp. 8⅜ × 11¼. (Available in U.S. only) 25682-0 Pa. **$11.95**

THE FUGUES ON THE MAGNIFICAT FOR ORGAN OR KEYBOARD, Johann Pachelbel. 94 pieces representative of Pachelbel's magnificent contribution to keyboard composition; can be played on the organ, harpsichord or piano. 100pp. 9 × 12. (Available in U.S. only) 25037-7 Pa. **$6.95**

MY LADY NEVELLS BOOKE OF VIRGINAL MUSIC, William Byrd. 42 compositions in modern notation from 1591 ms. For any keyboard instrument. 245pp. 8⅛ × 11. 22246-2 Pa. **$12.50**

ELIZABETH ROGERS HIR VIRGINALL BOOKE, edited with calligraphy by Charles J. F. Cofone. All 112 pieces from noted 1656 manuscript, most never before published. Composers include Thomas Brewer, William Byrd, Orlando Gibbons, etc. 125pp. 9 × 12. 23138-0 Pa. **$10.95**

THE FITZWILLIAM VIRGINAL BOOK, edited by J. Fuller Maitland, W. B. Squire. Famous early 17th-century collection of keyboard music, 300 works by Morley, Byrd, Bull, Gibbons, etc. Modern notation. Total of 938pp. 8⅜ × 11. Two-vol. set. 21068-5, 21069-3 Pa. **$31.90**

GREAT KEYBOARD SONATAS, Series I and Series II, Domenico Scarlatti. 78 of the most popular sonatas reproduced from the G. Ricordi edition edited by Alessandro Longo. Total of 320pp. 8⅜ × 11¼.
Series I 24996-4 Pa. **$7.95**
Series II 25003-2 Pa. **$7.95**

SONATAS AND FANTASIES FOR THE PIANO, W. A. Mozart, edited by Nathan Broder. Finest, most accurate edition, based on autographs and earliest editions. 19 sonatas, plus Fantasy and Fugue in C, K.394, Fantasy in C Minor, K.396, Fantasy in D Minor, K.397. 352pp. 9 × 12. (Available in U.S. only) 25417-8 Pa. **$14.95**

COMPLETE PIANO SONATAS, Joseph Haydn. 52 sonatas reprinted from authoritative Breitkopf & Härtel edition. Extremely clear and readable; ample space for notes, analysis. 464pp. 9⅜ × 12¼.
24726-0 Pa. **$10.95**
24727-9 Pa. **$10.95**

BAGATELLES, RONDOS AND OTHER SHORTER WORKS FOR PIANO, Ludwig van Beethoven. Most popular and most performed shorter works, including Rondo a capriccio in G and Andante in F. Breitkopf & Härtel edition. 128pp. 9⅜ × 12¼. 25392-9 Pa. **$8.95**

COMPLETE VARIATIONS FOR SOLO PIANO, Ludwig van Beethoven. Contains all 21 sets of Beethoven's piano variations, including the extremely popular *Diabelli Variations, Op. 120.* 240pp. 9⅜ × 12¼. 25188-8 Pa. **$11.95**

COMPLETE PIANO SONATAS, Ludwig van Beethoven. All sonatas in fine Schenker edition, with fingering, analytical material. One of best modern editions. 615pp. 9 × 12. Two-vol. set. (Available in U.S. only) 23134-8, 23135-6 Pa. **$23.90**

COMPLETE SONATAS FOR PIANOFORTE SOLO, Franz Schubert. All 15 sonatas. Breitkopf and Härtel edition. 293pp. 9⅜ × 12¼. 22647-6 Pa. **$12.95**

DANCES FOR SOLO PIANO, Franz Schubert. Over 350 waltzes, minuets, landler, ecossaises, other charming, melodic dance compositions reprinted from the authoritative Breitkopf & Härtel edition. 192pp. 9⅜ × 12¼. 26107-7 Pa. **$8.95**

Dover Piano and Keyboard Editions

Dover Piano and Keyboard Editions

SHORTER WORKS FOR PIANOFORTE SOLO, Franz Schubert. All piano music except Sonatas, Dances, and a few unfinished pieces. Contains Wanderer, Impromptus, Moments Musicals, Variations, Scherzi, etc. Breitkopf and Härtel edition. 199pp. 9⅜ × 12¼. 22648-4 Pa. **$9.95**

WALTZES AND SCHERZOS, Frédéric Chopin. All of the Scherzos and nearly all (20) of the Waltzes from the authoritative Paderewski edition. Editorial commentary. 214pp. 9 × 12. (Available in U.S. only) 24316-8 Pa. **$9.95**

COMPLETE PRELUDES AND ETUDES FOR SOLO PIANO, Frédéric Chopin. All 26 Preludes, all 27 Etudes by greatest composer of piano music. Authoritative Paderewski edition. 224pp. 9 × 12. (Available in U.S. only) 24052-5 Pa. **$8.95**

COMPLETE BALLADES, IMPROMPTUS AND SONATAS, Frédéric Chopin. The four Ballades, four Impromptus and three Sonatas. Authoritative Paderewski edition. 240pp. 9 × 12. (Available in U.S. only) 24164-5 Pa. **$9.95**

NOCTURNES AND POLONAISES, Frédéric Chopin. 19 *Nocturnes* and 16 *Polonaises* reproduced from the authoritative Paderewski Edition for pianists, students, and musicologists. Commentary. viii + 272pp. 9 × 12. (Available in U.S. only) 24564-0 Pa. **$10.95**

COMPLETE MAZURKAS, Frédéric Chopin. 51 best-loved compositions, reproduced directly from the authoritative Kistner edition edited by Carl Mikuli. 160pp. 9 × 12. 25548-4 Pa. **$8.95**

FANTASY IN F MINOR, BARCAROLLE, BERCEUSE AND OTHER WORKS FOR SOLO PIANO, Frédéric Chopin. 15 works, including one of the greatest of the Romantic period, the Fantasy in F Minor, Op. 49, reprinted from the authoritative German edition prepared by Chopin's student, Carl Mikuli. 224pp. 8⅝ × 11¼. 25950-1 Pa. **$7.95**

COMPLETE HUNGARIAN RHAPSODIES FOR SOLO PIANO, Franz Liszt. All 19 Rhapsodies reproduced directly from an authoritative Russian edition. All headings, footnotes translated to English. Best one volume edition available. 224pp. 8⅝ × 11¼. 24744-9 Pa. **$9.95**

ANNÉES DE PÈLERINAGE, COMPLETE, Franz Liszt. Authoritative Russian edition of piano masterpieces: *Première Année (Suisse): Deuxième Année (Italie)* and *Venezia e Napoli; Troisième Année,* other related pieces. 288pp. 9⅜ × 12¼. 25627-8 Pa. **$11.95**

COMPLETE ETUDES FOR SOLO PIANO, Series I: Including the Transcendental Etudes, Franz Liszt, edited by Busoni. Also includes Etude in 12 Exercises, 12 Grandes Etudes and Mazeppa. Breitkopf & Härtel edition. 272pp. 8⅝ × 11¼. 25815-7 Pa. **$11.95**

COMPLETE ETUDES FOR SOLO PIANO, Series II: Including the Paganini Etudes and Concert Etudes, Franz Liszt, edited by Busoni. Also includes Morceau de Salon, Ab Irato. Breitkopf & Härtel edition. 192pp. 8⅝ × 11¼. 25816-5 Pa. **$9.95**

SONATA IN B MINOR AND OTHER WORKS FOR PIANO, Franz Liszt. One of Liszt's most performed piano masterpieces, with the six Consolations, ten *Harmonies poetiques et religieuses,* two Ballades and two Legendes. Breitkopf and Härtel edition. 208pp. 8⅝ × 11¼. 26182-4 Pa. **$8.95**

PIANO TRANSCRIPTIONS FROM FRENCH AND ITALIAN OPERAS, Franz Liszt. Virtuoso transformations of themes by Mozart, Verdi, Bellini, other masters, into unforgettable music for piano. Published in association with American Liszt Society. 247pp. 9 × 12. 24273-0 Pa. **$11.95**

COMPLETE PIANO TRANSCRIPTIONS FROM WAGNER'S OPERAS, Franz Liszt. 15 brilliant compositions (1842–1882) on themes from *Rienzi, Flying Dutchman, Tannhäuser, Lohengrin,* other Wagnerian favorites. 176pp. 9 × 12. 24126-2 Pa. **$8.95**

COMPLETE WORKS FOR PIANOFORTE SOLO, Felix Mendelssohn. Breitkopf and Härtel edition of Capriccio in F# Minor, Sonata in E Major, Fantasy in F# Minor, Three Caprices, Songs without Words, and 20 other works. Total of 416pp. 9⅜ × 12¼. Two-vol. set. 23136-4, 23137-2 Pa. **$21.90**

COMPLETE SONATAS AND VARIATIONS FOR SOLO PIANO, Johannes Brahms. All sonatas, five variations on themes from Schumann, Paganini, Handel, etc. Vienna Gesellschaft der Musikfreunde edition. 178pp. 9 × 12. 22650-6 Pa. **$8.95**

COMPLETE SHORTER WORKS FOR SOLO PIANO, Johannes Brahms. All solo music not in other two volumes. Waltzes, Scherzo in E Flat Minor, Eight Pieces, Rhapsodies, Fantasies, Intermezzi, etc. Vienna Gesellschaft der Musikfreunde. 180pp. 9 × 12. 22651-4 Pa. **$8.95**

COMPLETE TRANSCRIPTIONS, CADENZAS AND EXERCISES FOR SOLO PIANO, Johannes Brahms. Vienna Gesellschaft der Musikfreunde edition, vol. 15. Studies after Chopin, Weber, Bach; gigues, sarabandes; 10 Hungarian dances, etc. 178pp. 9 × 12. 22652-2 Pa. **$9.95**

PIANO MUSIC OF ROBERT SCHUMANN, Series I, edited by Clara Schumann. Major compositions from the period 1830–39; *Papillons,* Toccata, Grosse Sonate No. 1, *Phantasiestücke, Arabeske, Blumenstück,* and nine other works. Reprinted from Breitkopf & Härtel edition. 274pp. 9⅜ × 12¼. 21459-1 Pa. **$12.95**

PIANO MUSIC OF ROBERT SCHUMANN, Series II, edited by Clara Schumann. Major compositions from period 1838–53; *Humoreske, Novelletten,* Sonate No. 2, 43 *Clavierstücke für die Jugend,* and six other works. Reprinted from Breitkopf & Härtel edition. 272pp. 9⅜ × 12¼. 21461-3 Pa. **$12.95**

PIANO MUSIC OF ROBERT SCHUMANN, Series III, edited by Clara Schumann. All solo music not in other two volumes, including *Symphonic Etudes, Phantaisie,* 13 other choice works. Definitive Breitkopf & Härtel edition. 224pp. 9⅜ × 12¼. 23906-3 Pa. **$10.95**

PIANO MUSIC 1888–1905, Claude Debussy. Deux Arabesques, Suite Bergamesque, Masques, first series of Images, etc. Nine others, in corrected editions. 175pp. 9⅜ × 12¼. 22771-5 Pa. **$7.95**

COMPLETE PRELUDES, Books 1 and 2, Claude Debussy. 24 evocative works that reveal the essence of Debussy's genius for musical imagery, among them many of the composer's most famous piano compositions. Glossary of French terms. 128pp. 8⅝ × 11¼. 25970-6 Pa. **$6.95**

PRELUDES, BOOK 1: The Autograph Score, Claude Debussy. Superb facsimile reproduced directly from priceless autograph score in Pierpont Morgan Library in New York. New Introduction by Roy Howat. 48pp. 8⅞ × 11. 25549-2 Pa. **$8.95**

PIANO MASTERPIECES OF MAURICE RAVEL, Maurice Ravel. Handsome affordable treasury; *Pavane pour une infante defunte, jeux d'eau, Sonatine, Miroirs,* more. 128pp. 9 × 12. 25137-3 Pa. **$6.95**

COMPLETE LYRIC PIECES FOR PIANO, Edvard Grieg. All 66 pieces from Grieg's ten sets of little mood pictures for piano, favorites of generations of pianists. 224pp. 9⅜ × 12¼. 26176-X Pa. **$10.95**

*Available from your music dealer or write for **free** Music Catalog to Dover Publications, Inc., Dept. MUBI, 31 East 2nd Street, Mineola, N.Y. 11501.*